S0-BHX-665

American Lives

Andrew Jackson

Rick Burke

DISCARDED

Heinemann Library
Chicago, Illinois

Public Library
Incorporated 1862
Barrie, Ontario

© 2003 Heinemann Library
a division of Reed Elsevier Inc.
Chicago, Illinois

Customer Service 888-454-2279

Visit our website at www.heinemannlibrary.com

All rights reserved. No part of this publication
may be reproduced or transmitted in any form or
by any means, electronic or mechanical, including
photocopying, recording, taping, or any information
storage and retrieval system, without permission in
writing from the publisher.

Created by the publishing team
at Heinemann Library

Designed by Ginkgo Creative, Inc.
Photo Research by Kathryn Creech
Printed and Bound in the United States by
Lake Book Manufacturing, Inc.

07 06 05 04 03
10 9 8 7 6 5 4 3 2 1

Acknowledgments
The author and publishers are grateful to the
following for permission to reproduce copyright
material: p. 4 Archivo Iconigrafico, S.A./Corbis; p. 5
Corbis; pp. 6, 9, 10, 11, 12, 13, 16, 17, 21, 22, 23
The Granger Collection, New York; p. 8 Archiving
Early America; p. 14 Historic Salisbury Foundation;
pp. 15, 25 The Library of Congress; pp. 18, 24
North Wind Picture Archives; pp. 19, 27 Bettmann/
Corbis; p. 29 Dave G. Houser/Corbis

Cover photograph: Archivo Iconografico,
S.A./Corbis

Special thanks to Patrick Halladay for his help in
the preparation of this book. Rick Burke thanks
Anne Marie . . . Andrew had his Rachel, and luckily
I have you.

Every effort has been made to contact copyright
holders of any material reproduced in this book.
Any omissions will be rectified in subsequent
printings if notice is given to the publisher.

Library of Congress Cataloging-in-Publication Data
Burke, Rick, 1957-
  Andrew Jackson / Rick Burke.
    v. cm. — (American lives)
Includes bibliographical references and index.
Contents: Andrew Jackson — Family — Childhood — Revolutionary War —
Elizabeth — Andrew's move — Dueling — The War of 1812 — The Battle of New
Orleans — Jackson becomes president — First days as president — Being
president — Jackson remembered.
  ISBN 1-40340-156-X (lib. bdg.) — ISBN 1-40340-412-7 (pbk.)
  1. Jackson, Andrew, 1767-1845—Juvenile literature. 2.
Presidents—United States—Biography—Juvenile literature. [1. Jackson,
Andrew, 1767-1845. 2. Presidents.] I. Title.
  E382 .B95 2002
  973.5'6'092—dc21
                        2002004143

Some words are shown in bold, **like this.** You can
find out what they mean by looking in the glossary.

For more information on the image of Andrew Jackson
that appears on the cover of this book, turn to page 4.

Contents

Andrew Jackson

From 1829 to 1837, Andrew Jackson was the seventh president of the United States. Jackson was loved by the citizens of the United States because he cared about what happened to the poorer people there.

He was born on March 15, 1767, in either South or North Carolina. No one knows for sure. Jackson himself had always been told that he was born in the Waxhaw **settlement** in South Carolina.

At the time Jackson was born, America was a **colony** of Great Britain. Jackson fought in two wars to be free from Great Britain's rule.

This picture of Andrew Jackson was painted in 1845 by Thomas Sully.

This drawing shows where Andrew was born.
He was the first president to grow up in a log cabin.

Before Jackson, presidents had come from wealthier families. Jackson was born poor, but through hard work he became rich.

Jackson's whole family died when he was a teenager, leaving him all alone in the world. But he still went on to lead his country. He became one of the greatest presidents in the history of the United States. Jackson said he was president for all people, not just for those who voted for him. He **represented** everyone.

Family

Andrew's parents were **immigrants** from Ireland who were looking for a better life in North America. Andrew's father moved to America because he had heard there was a lot of land available.

Andrew never knew his father. His father died in a farming accident just days before Andrew was born. It was almost impossible for Andrew's mother to make enough money by herself to buy food and clothes for her family.

The ships that immigrants took to America were usually crowded.

The Life of Andrew Jackson

1767	1797	1815	1821
Born on March 15 in the Waxhaw settlement.	Elected to United States **Congress.**	Led the United States army in the Battle of New Orleans.	Became first **governor** of Florida.

Andrew's brothers Hugh and Robert and their mother, Elizabeth, started living on the farm of the Crawfords, who were Andrew's aunt and uncle. Andrew had been born there.

The farm was in the Waxhaw **settlement.** The settlement was located near where the states of North and South Carolina meet today.

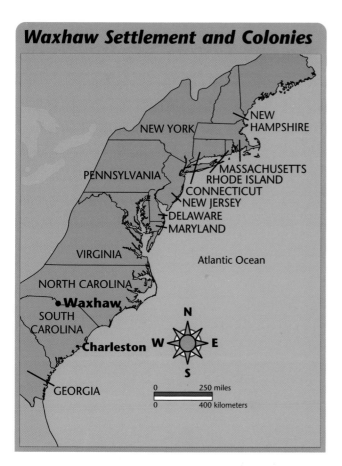

Waxhaw Settlement and Colonies

Hugh

Hugh, Andrew's sixteen-year-old brother, fought in the Battle of Stono Ferry in the **Revolutionary War.** *He died after the battle.*

1828	1832	1845
Elected president of the United States.	*Reelected president.*	*Died on June 8 at the Hermitage in Nashville, Tennessee.*

Childhood

Not everyone went to school where Andrew lived. Families needed their children to work to put food on the table and buy things.

Reading

In 1776, when Andrew was nine years old, he read the **Declaration of Independence** *to his neighbors.*

Hugh and Robert worked on their uncle's farm, but Elizabeth wanted Andrew to grow up to be a **minister.** She wanted him to get as much education as possible. Andrew didn't like school, but he was a good reader.

The newspapers that Andrew read looked like this one from Boston.

When Andrew was a boy, newspapers were printed in shops like the one in this picture.

News of what was happening in the **colonies** and around the world wasn't always easy to get when Andrew was growing up. People got most of their information from reading newspapers. They came from bigger cities and from England.

People who had newspapers shared them with their neighbors. When the newspapers got to the Waxhaw area, the townspeople would gather in an area in the town and listen to someone read the news. Andrew was often picked to read the news.

Revolutionary War

America became an independent country after the **Revolutionary War,** which began in 1775. Andrew wanted to join the army and help the **colonists** win freedom from Great Britain. But his mother told him that he was too young to fight.

Andrew was thirteen when he and Robert joined the **militia** in 1780, when the war was almost over. The militia was a group of soldiers from the same area. They learned how to shoot and march together.

The Battle of Lexington on April 19, 1775, was one of the first battles of the war.

This painting from 1876 shows when a soldier hit Andrew with a sword.

The next year, Andrew and Robert were captured by the British and held as prisoners.

Once, a British soldier ordered Andrew to clean the soldier's muddy boots. When Andrew refused, the soldier raised his sword and tried to hit Andrew in the head. Andrew ducked and raised his arm to protect his face. The sword made a deep cut on his forehead and fingers.

Andrew's Scar

Andrew had a scar on his forehead from when a British soldier cut him with a sword. Most paintings of Andrew as an adult don't show the scar.

Elizabeth

While prisoners, Robert and Andrew caught **smallpox.** Their mother, Elizabeth, helped them get out of prison. She had the American army trade British prisoners for her boys.

Elizabeth brought two horses from the farm to bring her sons back. She rode one horse and Robert rode the other. Andrew had to walk the 45 miles (72 kilometers) back home barefoot because he had lost his boots. Robert died the day after they reached the farm. Andrew almost died, but his mother cared for him until he was healthy.

Andrew's mother helped sick prisoners like the ones in this picture.

After Andrew got better, Elizabeth went to the city of Charleston, South Carolina, to help sick American prisoners. While she was helping the sick, Elizabeth caught **cholera** and died. With his entire family now dead, Andrew, at fourteen, was an **orphan.** Later in life, Andrew said he felt totally alone when he lost his family.

This painting shows British ships in the harbor of Charleston, South Carolina, shortly before the war began.

Andrew's Move

One of Andrew's grandfathers in Ireland died and left him 300 **British pounds,** which was a lot of money at the time. Andrew spent it all on nice clothes and making bets on games. He learned that he would have to be smarter with his money in the future.

When Andrew was seventeen, he rode to Salisbury, North Carolina, to study law in the office of Spruce Macay. People didn't have to go to college to learn how to be a lawyer back then. They could learn how by helping a lawyer do his work. Andrew became a lawyer, and in 1788 he moved to Nashville, Tennessee, to start his new job.

Andrew used this desk when he was learning about law. The desk is in a museum in Salisbury.

Rachel, pictured here, had moved to Tennessee when she was twelve years old.

The move to Nashville was good for Andrew. He was a good lawyer and later became a judge. He also met Rachel Donelson Robards. She was the daughter of the woman who ran a boardinghouse where Andrew lived. In this kind of house, a family rents out bedrooms and provides meals.

Rachel was married to a man named Lewis Robards, but he treated her badly. She **divorced** Robards and married Andrew in 1791. They were married for 37 years.

Jackson's Family

Rachel's brother let Andrew and Rachel adopt one of his twin boys. Andrew named the boy Andrew Jackson Junior.

Dueling

During Andrew's lifetime, men sometimes settled arguments by **dueling.** Two men would fight with swords or guns when they got mad at each other.

Charles Dickinson was the **son-in-law** of a man who lost money to Andrew in a bet. Dickinson said some mean things about Rachel. He also called Andrew a coward. Andrew challenged Dickinson to a duel with guns. Andrew's anger might have made him act too quickly. Many people thought Dickinson was the best shot in Tennessee.

This drawing shows Andrew's duel with Dickinson on May 30, 1806. Dickinson fell down when he was shot. He later died.

Guns like the ones in this picture were used in the duel.

Dickinson shot first and hit Andrew in the chest. Andrew put one hand over his wound to stop the bleeding. He then raised his gun and shot Dickinson.

Someone asked Andrew after the duel if he made a mistake by letting Dickinson shoot first. Andrew said he would have killed Dickinson no matter what.

Because the bullet was so close to Andrew's heart, his doctor felt that it wasn't safe to remove it. Andrew spent the rest of his life with the bullet in his chest.

The War of 1812

The United States fought another war with Great Britain beginning in 1812. The United States was young and not yet as strong as other countries. The British government didn't respect the government of the United States, even though Great Britain had lost the **Revolutionary War.** That made the leaders of the United States very angry.

One reason the two countries went to war again was because the British had forts along the western territory of the United States. The British leaders encouraged Indians to attack American **settlers** there.

British soldiers attacked an American fort in Ohio during the war, but they lost the fight.

This picture shows two British sailors with a group of American sailors who have been forced to work.

The British navy had also been capturing American sailors and forcing them to work on British ships. The leaders of the United States knew the country was not as powerful as Great Britain, but they were tired of being picked on. They decided to go to war with Great Britain again.

Andrew had been a general in the **militia** of Tennessee since 1802. When the war started, he offered to lead soldiers into battle.

The Battle of New Orleans

At first, the United States soldiers lost many battles. It was important for the Americans to protect the city of New Orleans, Louisiana. Food and other goods were shipped from and arrived at New Orleans.

The War Was Over

Because news traveled so slowly in Andrew's time, no one knew at the Battle of New Orleans that the war was already over. The leaders of the U.S. and Great Britain had agreed to stop fighting in December 1814.

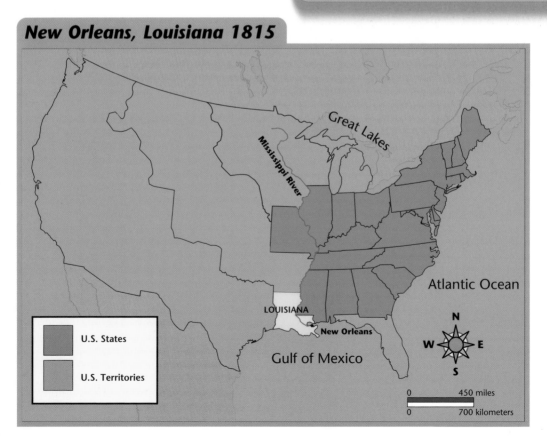

New Orleans, Louisiana 1815

Great Lakes

Mississippi River

Atlantic Ocean

LOUISIANA

New Orleans

Gulf of Mexico

N
W   E
S

U.S. States

U.S. Territories

0   450 miles
0   700 kilometers

In this painting, Andrew's army is shown shooting at British soldiers in the distance.

Andrew was sent to New Orleans to lead an army. His job was to stop the British from taking over the city. He was picked because he had experience fighting in the **militia.** As he marched, Andrew had to gather men who were willing to fight. His army was made up of farmers, Indians, former slaves, and pirates.

In January 1815, the two armies met in the Battle of New Orleans. Andrew's army had fewer men, but they still won the battle. It was the greatest victory of the war for the United States.

Jackson Becomes President

Andrew Jackson became a hero because of the Battle of New Orleans. He went back to Washington, D.C., as a member of **Congress** for Tennessee. He had first served there in 1796.

Florida

*After Spain sold Florida to the United States, Andrew became Florida's first **governor** in 1821. However, he only kept the job for a few months.*

In 1824, Jackson wanted to be the country's leader instead of leading an army. He decided to try to get elected president of the United States.

The U.S. Congress meets in the Capitol building in Washington, D.C. This picture shows how it looked in 1837.

John Quincy Adams was the sixth president of the United States.

More people voted for Jackson than the other men who wanted to be president. But because of special election rules, government leaders in Congress had to decide the election.

During the special election, the leaders picked John Quincy Adams to be president. Jackson thought he had been cheated. He tried again in 1828, and he beat Adams. He became the seventh president of the United States.

First Days as President

Jackson's wife, Rachel, didn't want him to be president. She was happy with their life at the Hermitage, their **plantation** in Nashville, Tennessee. One month after Jackson was elected president, Rachel died of a heart attack. Jackson went to Washington, D.C., by himself and missed Rachel for the rest of his life.

Jackson knew he could not have become president without the support of poor and common people. So he had a public party at the White House, which was then called the President's House, when he started his first **term.**

Jackson gave speeches on his way to Washington to start his presidency.

A lot of people came to celebrate when Jackson started his first term in 1829.

People came to celebrate, but they celebrated too much. The crowd broke furniture, plates, and glasses. At one point, Jackson had to climb out of a window in the President's House to get away from the crowd.

To get the crowd to leave, waiters brought big bowls of orange punch out onto the lawn. Once the crowd left the President's House to get some punch, the waiters locked the doors so people couldn't get back inside.

Being President

As president, Jackson wanted the national government to have more power than the states. He also believed that no one should keep a government job for his whole life. Jackson thought it was fairer for many different people to have a chance to work in government jobs.

Jackson lived well at the President's House and threw many parties. Fine foods were served, but usually Jackson liked a simple diet of bread, vegetables, rice, milk, and wine.

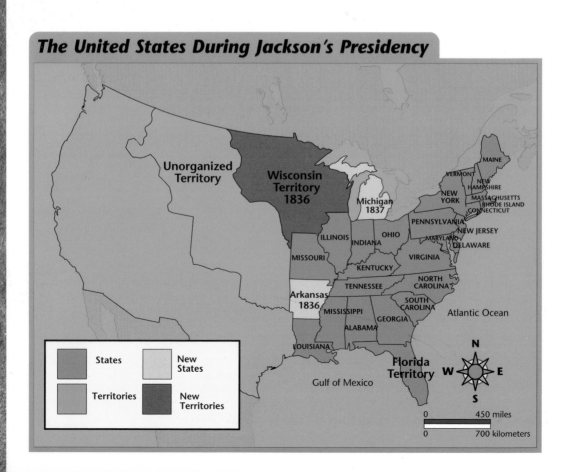

The United States During Jackson's Presidency

Unorganized Territory

Wisconsin Territory 1836

Michigan 1837

MAINE

VERMONT

NEW HAMPSHIRE

NEW YORK

MASSACHUSETTS

RHODE ISLAND

CONNECTICUT

PENNSYLVANIA

NEW JERSEY

ILLINOIS

OHIO

INDIANA

MARYLAND

DELAWARE

MISSOURI

VIRGINIA

KENTUCKY

NORTH CAROLINA

TENNESSEE

Arkansas 1836

SOUTH CAROLINA

MISSISSIPPI

GEORGIA

Atlantic Ocean

ALABAMA

LOUISIANA

Florida Territory

Gulf of Mexico

States

Territories

New States

New Territories

N W E S

0   450 miles
0   700 kilometers

After he was finished being president, Jackson returned to the Hermitage, his home in Nashville.

Presidents serve for four years. They must be reelected to continue being president. Jackson was reelected in 1832.

The United States was growing westward when Jackson was president. In the last years of his presidency, two new states became part of the country. Arkansas joined in June 1836, and Michigan joined in January 1837.

Jackson Firsts

- *First president to be born in a log cabin.*
- *First president to have served in both the* **Revolutionary War** *and the War of 1812.*
- *First president to ride on a train.*

Jackson Remembered

Jackson served the United States as president for two **terms.** He went back to live the last years of his life at the Hermitage. Jackson was sick his last few years. He was blind in one eye and almost deaf.

Trail of Tears

*When Jackson was president, **settlers** wanted to own land where Indian tribes lived. The Indians were forced by the government to sell their land and move to an area now known as the state of Oklahoma. Some made the whole trip by walking. Many became sick and died along the way. This journey is known as the Trail of Tears.*

He died on June 8, 1845. Jackson is buried next to Rachel in the gardens at the Hermitage.

Andrew Jackson is pictured on the U.S. $20 bill.

Andrew is known as a great leader because he gave the president more power in the U.S. government. Before Andrew's presidency, **Congress** was more powerful. Andrew thought the president should play a bigger part in deciding how the country was run.

Andrew looked out for what he thought was best for the common people of the country. He showed the nation that anyone, rich or poor, could grow up to be president.

About 200,000 people visit the Hermitage in Nashville each year.

Glossary

British pound money used in Great Britain. One pound is worth about $1.50 today.

cholera sickness that attacks the small intestines

colony group of people who move to another land but are still ruled by the country they moved away from. People who live in a colony are called colonists.

Congress main lawmaking group of the U.S. Includes the Senate and the House of Representatives.

Declaration of Independence document that said the United States was an independent nation. Independent means not being under the control or rule of another person or government.

divorce to end a marriage

dueling fighting between two people with swords or guns while other people watch

governor person who is elected to lead a state

immigrant person who moves from one country to another to live there for a long time

militia group of soldiers called to fight in an emergency

minister person who is the leader of a church

orphan child whose parents have died

plantation large farm on which one main crop is grown by workers who live there

represent to stand for

Revolutionary War war from 1775 to 1783 in which the American colonists won freedom from Great Britain

settlement new place or area where people live

settler person who goes to live in a new area

smallpox disease that causes fever and sores

son-in-law husband of a person's daughter

term length of time an elected official serves.
   The term of office for the president is four years.

More Books to Read

Potts, Steve. *Andrew Jackson: A Photo-Illustrated Biography*. Mankato, Minn.: Capstone Press, 1996.

Sabin, Louis. *Andrew Jackson, Frontier Patriot*. Mahwah, N.J.: Troll Communications, 1997.

Welsbacher, Anne. *Andrew Jackson*. Edina, Minn.: ABDO Publishing, 1999.

Places to Visit

The Hermitage
   4580 Rachel's Lane
   Nashville, Tennessee 37076-1344
   Visitor Information: (615) 889-2941

Museum of the Waxhaws
and Andrew Jackson Memorial
   8215 Waxhaw Highway
   Waxhaw, North Carolina 28173
   Visitor Information: (704) 843-1832

Index